YOU CAN BANK ON THAT BOOK 2

CREATIVE DISMISSAL

Brian L. Coventry

Author of: "Adopted at Age Four"
And
"You Can Bank On That   Book 1"

authorHOUSE®

AuthorHouse™ LLC
1663 Liberty Drive
Bloomington, IN 47403
www.authorhouse.com
Phone: 1-800-839-8640

Published by AuthorHouse 12/10/2013

ISBN: 978-1-4918-3593-7 (sc)
ISBN: 978-1-4918-3592-0 (e)

Library of Congress Control Number: 2013920734

Any people depicted in stock imagery provided by Thinkstock are models,
and such images are being used for illustrative purposes only.
Certain stock imagery © Thinkstock.

This book is printed on acid-free paper.

Because of the dynamic nature of the Internet, any web addresses or links contained in
this book may have changed since publication and may no longer be valid. The views
expressed in this work are solely those of the author and do not necessarily reflect the
views of the publisher, and the publisher hereby disclaims any responsibility for them.

This book is a work of fiction. People, places, events and situations are the
product of the author's imagination. Any resemblance to actual persons
living or dead, or historical events, is purely coincidental.

Dedicated to my late and much missed Father-in-law

He was more of a brother to me than the father of my wife.

What started out as fire and water ended up as two peas in a pod.

A constant reminder to us is on the front door of our home.

It's a wooden plaque engraved at Shediac, New Brunswick that reads:

"The House That Frank Built"

Every fool has a rainbow,
But he never seems to find
The reward that should be waiting
At the end of the line
And he'll give up a bed of roses for
A life filled with thorns
And go chasing after rainbows
Every time a dream is born . . . .
And every fool has a rainbow that only he can see
Every fool has a rainbow and the rule applies to me . . . .
Merle Haggard

PREFACE

Creative Dismissal. Also referred to as Constructive Dismissal or Constructive Discharge. It occurs when an employee resigns because their employer's behaviour has become so intolerable or heinous or made life so difficult that the employee has no choice but to resign. Since the resignation was not truly voluntary, it is in effect a termination. For example, when an employer makes life extremely difficult for an employee, to attempt to have the employee resign, the employer is trying to effect a constructive discharge.

When the employee hangs on, in spite of the torment and bad behavior of the employer, then there comes a point where the employer has to stop the intimidation and actually dismiss the employee and then is open to liability and legal action. This is much more costly than if the employee resigns in frustration. When this is the case (a frustrated resignation) all the resigning employee can receive is severance pay, vacation pay, loss of all benefits and any other minimal final payouts.

Constructive dismissal is usually caused by: unilateral contract changes by the employer (e.g: cuts in pay or status, even if temporary) refusal of holiday, dramatic changes to duties, hours or location (beyond reasonable travelling distance) bullying or swearing, criticizing in front of subordinates, lack of support (forcing to do two people's jobs) singling out for no pay raise or miniscule useless amounts after taxes.

An employee should always maintain off-site records of Performance Appraisals, local volunteer work that is done and any recognition of same as well as Letters of Appreciation and/or Approval from Head Office or his or her clients.

In the following story, there is a clear message that one must always be on the lookout for signs that some Head Office goon or Business Owner has painted a target on your back.

The expression that best suits when one reaches this point in his/her job is: "Better start wearing your knife-proof vest!!"

CHAPTER 1

The lunch had gone well right up to the time when Leslie's competitor and close friend started discussing "creative dismissal", a practice in vogue with Senior Management for getting rid of higher paid Branch Managers.

At that point Leslie lost his appetite. Brad, his lunch mate was only trying to forewarn him based on recent experiences his fellow Managers in the CIBC (Canadian Imperial Bank of Commerce) had been put through.

It was a typical midweek lunch meeting between two Branch Managers of competing Financial Institutions on the one hand CIBC, a federally chartered Bank and on the other a provincially chartered Caisse Populaire which is basically a Credit Union with Members. Both companies compete for the same business and normally competitors don't associate with each other. But in this case, both Leslie and Brad had met long ago at Chamber of Commerce luncheon meetings. What had started out as casual conversation at the food counter had eventually became a friendship based on mutual respect.

On this particular day, they had met for lunch at a popular Eatery operated by none other than the Mayor of North Bay, Mr. Kevin Ghattas, one of Leslie's client's at the Caisse Populaire.

Mayor Ghattas came over to their table as soon as they arrived and said: "Well, well, the two worst Bank Managers in North Bay are gracing my humble restaurant."

I winked at my friend and said:" You know Kevin, us two guys are pretty popular in town. Pretty high profile. We're actually thinking one of us should challenge you in the next election for that prestigious Mayor's job of yours . . . ."

We saw him lose his composure for a nanosecond and then we all started to laugh at the same time.

"You guys, go and eat and leave me alone . . . . Hahaha! . . ."

After we sat down with our plates filled to overflowing, Brad all of a sudden got serious. He said: "I like you Les, but I think I want to bring you up to speed on some information I received recently. You're kind of on a roll right now aren't you?"

"Where are you going with this?" I said . . .

"Well, we all know you can be a hero today and the asshole of the Bank tomorrow, right?"

I said: "Well, yes to a certain extent, but if you cover your ass and work hard and get the results, why worry?"

Brad said: "I've got a buddy down in Toronto, works in a Branch on University Avenue. Always got great results, for over twenty years. Last year, he had been in the Bank in one capacity or another for 24 years and he didn't quite make his targets in volume and profit for his last fiscal year. First time in those twenty years at that Branch."

He continued:"One morning he showed up for work a half hour late, he'd stopped at a client's business to get some paperwork signed. When he got to the Branch the Head Office suits were sitting in his office. He wasn't ready for the trip they laid on him. They have this down to a science these HR goons. They blindside you saying you are not performing up to our expectations or the Bank has decided in our restructuring phase now in progress that your Managerial Level is not required in this market or we are prepared to offer you a desk job in Vancouver Head Office in the Credit Department (the only position currently open with your background or training) or we can offer you this exit package."

"So he freaked. You can imagine the thoughts exploding in his brain at this point. You know? What about my 15 year old daughter in high school, getting ready for college? How do I explain this to my wife Eleanor, we never ever thought my job wasn't safe? How do I explain this to my parents, her parents, my Bank customers?

So they slide this piece of crap offer to buy him out for X dollars if he just leaves quietly. At first glance it appears generous, but it is far short of what he should really receive based on years of service, profitability he made for the Bank and its shareholders. But he's so freaked out he grabs the pen and signs it. At that point he was screwed. He could have negotiated at least double if not triple their original offer if he'd refused to sign their deal and got a decent Labour Relations Lawyer."

At this point I started to find I'd lost my appetite.

"Why are you telling me all this?" I said.

"Because, Leslie, I'm almost in exactly the same situation as my buddy. Doing great now for close to twenty years. But after his deal, I am going to keep copies of all my PA's off site at home or in my safety deposit box. I'm also going to keep notes of every conversation I have with these Head Office HR dickheads. I don't trust any one of them."

I said: "Well I don't know. Last month the Mayor wrote a letter to our Ontario Senior Vice-President and said to him don't ever transfer Swartman out of North Bay. We love this guy, we want him to be the Manager of that Caisse Populaire Branch until he's ready to retire.

Th e VP wrote him back and said the usual stuff, we are very pleased you are happy with our man on the job. Then he said we will keep him there into his Golden Years . . . I can show you the memo, man."

"Doesn't mean dick-all" said Brad.

"What do you mean by that?"

"C'mon Les. These VP's come and go every couple of years. His promises or undertakings aren't grandfathered into his replacement!

Get a grip! If you can't see the benefit of what I'm saying, for God's sake at least start copying your PA's and letters like that from your VP and squirreling them off site. Anything that says you're doing a good job, stuff in the newspaper, your participation in the Chamber of Commerce, anything that is positive stuff ."

"OK ,OK". I said. "Maybe you're right. A little covering your ass doesn't hurt even if you're on a roll considering your chum's story.

Maybe next year will be a flop, who knows?"

"Exactly man . . . ."

We wrapped up our meeting and I went back to the Branch with the first time in a long time a really uneasy feeling in my gut. I would start to watch for the signs of "Creative Dismissal". This is when the Head office honchos paint a target on your back and decide to make your life miserable to the extent that you will quit and spare them the need to "package you off ". I knew all about it. I had done it with non-performing employees myself. There were no Unions in the Bank so they couldn't complain to their shop steward and we had a graduated system to eliminate sub-standard performers.

Little did I know the events to unfold in the next decade or so that made my lunch with Brad from the CIBC the best one hour I ever spent with a "friendly competitor."

CHAPTER 2

Back in the Branch I was thinking a lot about the conversation I'd had and the fact that Unions were taboo in the Canadian Banking System. I recalled a conversation I had on this very subject with a buddy of mine in Ottawa that worked at a Branch of BMO (Bank of Montreal) in Ottawa: It went something like this:

"Marcel, has there ever been a branch try to Unionize in BMO?

Marcel said: "Oh yeah. Oh yeah. Down in the town of Bon Appetite, Quebec. "There was this Assistant Accountant in that Branch. He thought he was the best thing since sliced bread. Only he was only OK, not the big deal he thought he was. Anyway, he keeps getting passed over for the promotion to Accountant job. After a couple years he gets upset about his lack of promotions and started talking to a Union rep in town who puts the bug in his ear to get the Branch unionized. Next thing you know he's meeting all the clerical staff off-site and talking them into this Union thing. But the Branch Management aren't stupid. They know what's going on.

So the next Monday morning, when everyone showed up for work, there's the Regional Vice President and three HR people sitting in the Manager's office, having a coffee.

A staff meeting is called and the Branch Manager explains that Monsieur Guy Lafontaine, Regional Vice President would like to have a few words with the staff. The Meeting went something like this:

"Good Morning, Ladies and Gentleman. I have reviewed with interest the history of our Branch here in Bon Appetite, Quebec and we have served this community very well for over 75 years. We are confident that we have very good Management employees running our day to day operations and that our clerical staff are doing a satisfactory job. Unfortunately we have some very grave concerns about the recent developments that suggest that the non-management employees are considering unionizing the Branch.

Sorry, people. This is not going to happen. As of today, this Branch is closed down and all our business in this town will be transferred to the nearby Town of Sacre Mere de Couer. Your clients will either travel the 26 miles to our Branch in Sacre Mere de Couer or they will deal with the Caisse Populaire Desjardins or the Banque Royale in Jacquesville. All clerical employees are hereby terminated and you are required to clean out all your personal possessions from the Branch after this meeting and leave the premises. You will receive your ROE (Record of Employment) in the mail in a few days.

Please commence withdrawing your personal effects immediately as we have a Moving Van scheduled to arrive by 10:00 a.m. We are in the process of posting a sign on the front door: "BRANCH CLOSED UNTIL FURTHER NOTICE".

If you have any questions: Messers. Gagne, Charron and Vigneault are hear to answer your questions from our Human Resources Department."

And so ended the unionizing of BMO, Bon Appetite, Quebec. Any other Branch in Quebec (or anywhere else for that matter) had an immediate taste of what was in store for them if they even considered unionizing anywhere.

On the other hand, the Banks, Trust Companies, Credit Unions and Caisse Populaires were providing salaries and benefits that were well in line with unionized companies. But they ruled their organizations with an iron fist.

No Unions!

That message loud and clear throughout the Industry.

In Canada, the Financial Services Industry exists to make a profit and to provide a good return on Investment to their shareholders.

So it is a tremendous balancing act keeping clients, employees and shareholders all happy or at least comfortable with their results year after year.

Canada has the strongest Banking system on the globe and I have always believed it was because the Unions haven't managed to get their grips into the Financial Services Industry.

CHAPTER 3

Meanwhile Back at the Branch

We over the course of around three years moved our reputation in the community from that "Farmers Bank" or "that French Bank" to "Favourite Banking Institution" in North Bay and "Favourite Bank Tellers" and "Favourite Investment Advisors" in the annual North Bay Nugget survey of client satisfaction of many types of Retail, Service, and Professional providers.

This particular year we received three certificates from the North Bay Nugget and they were not only proudly displayed in our Branch where all the clients could see, but also the Certificates were published in the Newspaper with all the other winners in the other categories.

Needless to say, this was a source of pride both for the staff, our clients and my Head Office superiors.

I had my Senior Assistant Manager who handled all the mortgages, personal loans and trained new Credit Trainees. She had been in the Branch at this point over 20 years and knew just about everybody in North Bay. She was as I used to call her: "my walking talking encyclopedia".

A few days after I took over the Branch I called her in to ask her about a client who was on the overdraft report that day. I said: "Allison what do you know about this guy Jacques Gagnon. He's overdrawn in his chequeing account today?"

She says: " Mr.Swartman, you don't have to worry about this guy. He's the salt of the earth. Works full time as a mechanic at North Bay Chrysler now for 15 years. His wife Ginette she's a part-time RNA at North Bay District Hospital. They got 3 kids all gems and live out at the east end in a nice bungalow worth about $75,000 which is free and clear. All I can figure is he must have wrote a cheque he forgot about or didn't mark it in his book. His pay deposit is on Friday and he gets about $500 + after deductions."

So I said: "Allison what do you not know about this guy?"

Allison replies: "Not much, I can tell you what he and Ginette drive to work in and the ages of their three kids. Anything else you need to know?"

"No Allison, you are simply amazing! Thanks!"

"No problem Boss."

"Allison don't call me Mr. Swartman and don't call me Boss. From now on just call me Leslie."

"OK Leslie."

This type of conversation would happen frequently as I was using Allison's knowledge of our clients to fast track my knowledge and provide quicker responses to requests by these new customers I was getting used to.

Her total knowledge of our client base was however like a double edged sword. One day, she and I were in the vault and we were looking up the collateral file on a particular Commercial Client's loans with the Branch. In walked Pierrette, a junior teller holding a Visa application in her hand. She asked Ginette:

"Ginette, is it OK to fill in a Visa application with Michel Picotte?"

Ginette replied in a booming tone of voice: "That little Christ'er is getting no Visa from me or anywhere else for that matter! He's been the black sheep of the Picotte family ever since he got out of diapers. If he's not in trouble with the law, he's giving his poor mom and dad ulcers over some other problem. Tell him his application is declined. Period!"

She also had the goods on every staff member in the Branch and if I allowed her to continue sharing her knowledge of everyone and everything, I could easily spend an entire day. But I learned soon to get the bare facts I needed and then end the conversation quickly as I didn't need everyone's life history and hear about every shred of their "dirty laundry".

When I first arrived, I realized that my Branch Accountant was a rising star in The Caisse. It seemed I was only there a few weeks when his Transfer/Promotion to the Ottawa "Flagship Branch" came through. I asked is there anybody in the Branch ready or capable to replace him. He replied not yet, they will send in the Accountant in Sturgeon Falls for a while. There has been a chain reaction resulting in multiple transfers both in Ottawa and Northern Ontario.

He then suggested I keep my eye on Jennifer O'Grady, the Assistant Accountant. She was very well organized, a perfectionist and good with the clients, but on the shy side and needs to be brought out of her shell. But with training and encouragement in time could be groomed into a first-class Branch Accountant.

I made a mental note of that and followed up on that in the weeks and months ahead.

CHAPTER 4

MEANWHILE BACK AT THE HOMESTEAD

We were getting little things done payday by payday on our Maison Quebecois (which is like a Cape Cod style home one and a half stories with dormer windows) on the lake behind Anne's parents. Up until I was elevated to a Level 65 Manager with the corresponding salary increase, we weren't in a big hurry to get a mortgage.

But we finally decided, let's take the equity out of what we've got in here now and finish this 100% and quit living with a sand basement with vapor barrier blocking off the dampness rising from there. Let's put exterior finish on the outside, We're getting tired of looking at "black joe". How about real stairs up to the front door instead of the mickey mouse job I had thrown together with 2" x 6" boards assembled in a very unlevel but sturdy manner.

Barb's cousin kept asking if we wanted him to get started at the brick exterior finish. It would require no maintenance, insulate us from extreme weather and last forever. Plus add a great deal of value to the place instead of vinyl or wood siding.

I applied for a staff mortgage and asked if they would lend me 75% of the appraised value over 25 years amortization at a preferred staff rate. My boss in Ottawa rubber stamped my request and we proceeded with the Appraisal on an "as-is" current value and "as completely finished" value.

The Appraiser came and was quite impressed with the stage we were at. He also liked the location. We were facing the lake with a southern exposure and the scenery was quite impressive. Surrounded by mature white and red pines, maples and oak. We had a maple tree at the far edge of our lot that had to be 100 years old. It was huge, at least 5 feet thick at the base and over 80 feet tall. (In later years I would put 4 taps in it for maple syrup, every tap produced sap.)

In his summary, he stated quality of construction meets or exceeds building codes (thanks to my father-in-law Peter the perfectionist) at it's current stage it was 65% complete but at 100% complete it would be worth $115,000. Current value $74,750. Since I was approved for 75% of the current appraised value I could access $55,300.

We had ratcheted up our Credit cards to the limit, so the first thing we wanted to do was to pay them off. This took a $15,000 bite out of the $55 grand. Since this was an "equity take-out" not a Construction Mortgage we took the balance of the funds and put them in a daily interest account.

We then ordered a tandem load of gravel so we could get our basement finished.

It's a good thing we were still young and full of energy and enthusiasm! Because shoveling a tandem load of gravel with spades through basement windows is a monumental task. Took us well over a week. Then we had to go into the basement and spread all this gravel evenly throughout the entire area. Then the cement truck could come and put a layer of pre-mix over all that gravel. It had to cure for so many hours before the cement finisher came with his big machine and smoothed out the cement like one big cement block. It then had to cure for several hours, but we stripped the vapour barrier away as there was next to no humidity coming out of the basement when he was through.

Now we decided enough is enough. We wanted to get this thing done and over with. We were operating with the main floor bathroom never even considered putting in the upstairs bathroom. So we went to the Building Supply Store and ordered out Vanity, toilet and a whirlpool bathtub. Peter said he had already ran the plumbing up and capped it for when we were ready so he'd hook it up when they arrived.

Meanwhile I'd been in Ottawa for Manager meetings and I asked my former Italian client who he recommended for bathroom and kitchen mirrors, appliances etc. He sent me to Preston Hardware on Preston Street in Little Italy. They had mirrors, towel holders, toilet paper dispensers that you'd never see in a regular store like Sears or The Bay. (Made in Italy of course.)

I decided to bring Ann down to look at and approve if we should buy them. We'd combine the trip with a visit to my Aunts in the West End and maybe hit the Carlingwood or St.Laurent Malls.

Ann oo'd and aahd' about the equipment I wanted and kept on oo'ing and aah'ing about almost the entire store until I finally dragged her out after ordering our mirror, towel holders and toilet paper dispensers.

We would find out in subsequent years that while these were beautiful pieces of glass and chrome in later years they were not replaceable as the company in Italy went Bankrupt. Imagine that?

CHAPTER 5

Adoption Time had finally arrived

You would think that after fifteen years of applying to the Children's Aid that we would finally be offered a child to adopt. No Way. Actually Ann had a cousin in Eganville who knew of a girl who was pregnant with a second child out of wedlock. She already had a 3 year old daughter Esther who was taken into custody by Family & Children's Services and placed with the girl's Grandmother. This was because the mother was into both drugs and alcohol and wasn't considered fit to raise any child including the one placed with granny or the one on the way.

So the pregnant Mom decided and knew her best bet was to give up the child to a good family because granny said:" I can't take on a newborn at 65 years of age!"

Ann's cousin suggested that she knew of a childless couple that would like to adopt a child and would she like to meet them to see if she would approve of them.

This appealed to her as she had a certain amount of control. On the other hand, if she did nothing, Family & Children's Services would take her newborn and place it in a foster home.

So a meeting was set. The expectant mother had a lawyer in Eganville who would arrange a meeting with the potential adoptive parents. If she approved of them then the lawyer would co-ordinate the adoption between the FACS (Family and Children's Services) of Renfrew County and the Children's Aid Society of the District of Nippissing and Parry Sound.

We received a letter from the Eganville Lawyer asking us to phone and arrange a mutually convenient time to meet with the expectant mother and her lawyer.

We phoned and a meeting was scheduled for the following Wednesday in Eganville. I hadn't used my "floater" for that year so I exercised my option. (A floater is like an extra day off to take for personal reasons.) Meanwhile, I'd probably clocked several days in unpaid overtime so I didn't feel the slightest bit guilty to take this day off.

When we arrived at the Lawyer's office that next Wednesday there was only one person in the waiting room. She was a very short pretty young blonde girl obviously pregnant and blushed as we entered the room.

She said: "You must be the couple I'm supposed to meet? My name is Hannah." And she blushed again.

Mr. Wolfgang Klein, the Lawyer, appeared at his office door and invited us in.

There were very comfortable leather client chairs that we all sat in and he began the conversation.

He started: " This meeting is a simple informal occasion. Hannah here has decided to put up her child for adoption and she just wants to be sure it will be going to a good family. So, Hannah. Do you have any questions of Leslie or Ann? As I explained, we can only use first names during this meeting."

Hannah looked at both of us then asked: "Are you religious people?"

Ann replied: " We are both Catholic and attend Mass every Sunday."

Hannah asked: "Do you have any other children now?"

Ann decided she was going to field the questions woman to woman. So she replied:

"We are not able to have children because of reasons that effect both Leslie and myself. The Doctor's say in our case it will be impossible."

At this point, Hannah reached into one of her pockets and produced a picture of a young girl about three years old. Blonde hair, very pretty very Germanic features like her mother Hannah.

She said: "This is my daughter Bronwen. I had to give her up to her grandmother by the Family and Children Services because I've had drinking and drug abuse problems."

This visibly upset Ann. She asked: "Are you using alcohol or drugs while you are in your condition?"

Hannah replied: "No way! I stopped altogether for Bronwen and I've stopped altogether for this pregnancy too . . . ."

16

Ann looked relieved then asked if Hannah knew if it was a boy or a girl.

Hannah replied: "I don't know and I would rather not know. I've decided I should give this kid up to a good family and I'd rather just not have any more to know than necessary."

She then said: "Mr. Klein I don't have any more questions. I like Leslie and Ann, and I'm OK with the adoption."

Wolgang Klien said: " Not so fast Hannah, maybe you should think about this for a day or so then make your decision."

"Whatever you say. I doubt if I'll change my mind." Said Hannah.

Mr. Klein then asked: " Now do you have any questions of Hannah at this point?"

This is where I decided I should say something meaningful. I said: "I'm glad we had this meeting today. I just want you to know that your child, boy or girl will have a very loving mother and father and be brought into a great family. You have no worries about that, I guarantee . . ."

We looked over at Hannah and her eyes were tearing up, but she said: "I know. Thank you" Then she got up and left the room.

Mr. Wolfgang Klein said: "This was a good meeting. It went well. I'll be in touch." And he shook both our hands and we left and headed back home to North Bay.

The following day Mr. Klein called to say that Hannah was very impressed with us and was one hundred percent in favour of placing the child with us. Mr. Klein said since she is voluntarily starting the private adoption process, he would have to co-ordinate the interviews and adoption process through the social workers with Family and Children's Services Renfrew County and the Children's Aid society of the District of Nippissing and Parry Sound.

We were quite happy with that outcome and even happier the following day when we received a call from a Victor Budge, a Social Worker with the North Bay Children's Aid. He explained that the process involved a series of meetings, the first one in his office the next two in our home. The other two in our home would be where he got an idea of how we live, family dynamics, cleanliness and pride of ownership. And of course, our suitability as future parents.

The first meeting in his office was mainly filling in a huge number of forms and questionnaires, but what I sensed was that Mr. Budge was reading our body language and asking questions that provided him with conclusions he needed to reach. I knew that as I did it all the time in the Bank with both clients and employees.

Since Hannah was already in third trimester we had already started to turn our guest room into a future nursery. We had bought a special crib that would at first be in our Master Bedroom and moved into the Nursery later when we were comfortable not having the child in the same room. The nursery was next door to the master bedroom but we would start off probably being "over-protective".

Mr.Budge seemed very comfortable with us even at the first meeting and after that it seemed he was pretty much just going through the motions. He was already convinced we were very good candidates for parenthood.

About three days after our final third house meeting he called and told us his file was complete and he would forward it off to his office who in turn would send it to Renfrew County FACS and the mother's lawyer. He would be billing a fee of $120 which we were to pay to the Eganville Lawyer, not to be at the mother's expense. I told him I felt that this was way too little for all the work he had done and we would rather pay him more. He said that was all he was allowed to charge, this was voluntary work outside office hours and this was all they would allow him to charge.

So ended the interview process. Now it was just sit and wait.

Brian L. Coventry

CHAPTER 6

THE VERY NEXT DAY

Dr. Gerard Labelle was on vacation. He had been completely in the loop on the adoption and speaking with Hannah's Obstetrician in Eganville on a regular basis. He had brought another local GP, Mrs. Elaine Weatherby up to speed and asked her to handle things if the child was born during his absence. She happened to be married to one of my clients, a prominent lawyer in North Bay, Tom Grecco.

At 10:00 a.m. the two of them were standing at the counter peering into my office both looking like the cat that swallowed the cream. My Secretary let them in and the were seated. Dr.Weatherby spoke up immediately. She had a no-nonsense let's get straight to the point type of manner and said:

"Congratulations, Leslie. You are soon to become the father of a bouncing baby boy who entered this world at 2:35 a.m. at the St.Francis Memorial Hospital in Barry's Bay." She went on: " He weighed in at eight pounds six ounces and mother and child are fine. Except, they said he was diagnosed as having a "wet lung" so they transferred him immediately by ambulance to CHEO in Ottawa."

CHEO is the "Children's Hospital of Eastern Ontario."

She went on: " A wet lung is when the child is passing through the birth canal and asperates some fluids into the lungs. It's not really serious, but they aren't as equipped for this condition in Barry's Bay as they are at CHEO. Besides, your GP, Gerard was very concerned as was the Birth Mother's Doctor that this child should be tested as soon as possible for "Fetal Alcohol Syndrome". Apparently the mother kept vowing that she wasn't doing drugs or alcohol during the pregnancy, but she doesn't have a very good track record."

"So there you have it. What have you got to say, Leslie?"

Before I could answer Tom chipped in: "When was the last time you changed a baby's diaper, Les?" Big Grin.

"Never", I said.

I went on: "Well I am totally overwhelmed! So what do I do now? Am I to go see this little guy down in Ottawa or what? What do I tell Ann?"

Dr. Weatherby continued: " You are going to call CHEO today, ask for the Neo-Natal Unit. The Head Nurse knows that this is an adoption scenario and that you are the prospective adoptive parents. They will schedule an appointment for you and Ann to go down and see your son in the next day or so. By then the wet lung problem will be resolved plus a specialist will have determined if there is Fetal Alcohol Syndrome."

At this point I thought Elaine Weatherby had had a serious expression on her face but all of a sudden the dark clouds rolled in and with a very intense look on her face she stated: "Leslie, if this child has Fetal Alcohol Syndrome, I strongly suggest you two walk away from this adoption! I know how much you and Ann want a child, but a boy with this condition should be fostered by a family that can handle this type of disability."

At that point my stomach turned into complete knots and I was temporarily speechless.

When I finally refocused I said to Doctor Elaine: " Well he is being tested right? If the test comes out OK then it's a go, right? I'd rather not lay this trip on Ann at this point. We should cross that bridge when we come to it . . . . Right?"

"Yes, Leslie. I just want you to be aware that there are significant risks here that you need to know up front. That's all."

I said: "OK. I really appreciate you filling me in.

At this point they both stood up, shook my hand and said they hoped everything would work out for the good.

That knot in my gut wasn't getting any better . . . .

CHAPTER 7

Back at the home front.

I was dialing my home phone number before the door was even closed behind them. Ann answered after the second ring.

I told her everything in full detail except the part about my advice from Doctor Elaine.

I had been given the phone number of the Neo-Natal unit and told her I would call and see when we could go down for our first visit. Then I'd get back to her and we'd plan our trip to Ottawa.

I then called Ottawa, CHEO Neo-Natal unit nursing station. They had been advised the adoptive parents would be calling by the mother's Doctor in Eganville.

So when I identified myself the Nurse said: "Yes, Mr. Swartman we've been expecting your call!"

She went on: "There are a few things I can tell you right now, and we can book you in the day after tomorrow to see your little linebacker!!" Then she laughed.

"What do you mean by that?" I asked.

She replied: "You've probably never been in a Neo-Natal unit before, but just about every baby in here are pre-mature deliveries in the two to five pound range. Your boy takes up the entire crib at eight pounds six ounces and is very healthy and robust. By the way, they have determined there is no Wet Lung problem and other test are being performed tomorrow to determine any other possible problems, so we will have the results when you come down Wednesday, if that works for you . . . ."

"We'll be there with bells on. What time should we show up?"

"How's ten o'clock sound?"

"You got'er . . ."

" We'll see you and Mrs. Swartman then."

I then called Ann and we discussed the trip arrangements and I informed my Branch Accountant I would be taking Wednesday off as a floater for "family reasons". No big announcements until everything was one hundred percent certain for many reasons.

First of all, The Birth Mother could by law rescind her decision up to 30 days after the birth and reclaim the child. Secondly, we would have to make a major decision if the child was born with Fetal Alcohol Syndrome. We would be on pins and needles during the entire nerve racking process.

We informed Ann's Mom and Dad. Her mother was all excited but Peter seemed to hold back on the enthusiasm. I figured he probably wanted a son early in his marriage way back then, but that wasn't to be and since there was a chance his ability to have a grandson could blow up on him, he didn't want to get his hopes up.

Wednesday came. We didn't need an alarm clock. We were both up at the break of dawn preparing for the trip to Ottawa.

THE TRIP TO OTTAWA

CHEO is in the East end of Ottawa a short distance off the Queensway. It's a huge facility and devotes itself entirely to children and young adults. We were advised at the information desk how to get to the Neo-Natal Unit.

When we arrived at that floor we went directly to the Nurses Station and introduced ourselves.

"So you're the lucky couple who are adopting that handsome baby in there!" The Head Nurse said.

"Wait'll you see him. He wins the "baby beauty contest" hands down . . . no competition!"

She then explained that we had to don robes and wear face masks before entering the room. And paper slippers over our shoes.

As we entered the room we couldn't help but notice all the babies other than ours were like little dolls in incubators with tubes all over them, some not much bigger than my fist. They were all premature from 3 to 5 or 6 pounds. Our boy was like a linebacker for the Ottawa Rough Riders. He practically filled his incubator at close to 9 pounds. But he had all the tubes on as well. This concerned me.

I asked: "How come he's hooked up to all those tubes and monitors?"

The nurse replied: "Don't let that bother you. When he arrived there were specific concerns that he might have Fetal Alcohol Syndrome and Wet Lung. We have to monitor him closely in either event as part of the overall diagnosis. We have ruled out the Wet Lung, and after you have your visit with "Baby C" our resident specialist wants to talk to you about the test results on the Fetal Alcohol Syndrome."

"I'm not sure I like the sound of that . . ." I said.

"It's just that I'm not allowed to discuss this diagnosis with you, only the specialist himself." She said.

Anyway there he was, pink cheeks, wide awake smiling up at us like he already knew us and we were already acceptable in his eyes.

Ann asked: "Can we pick him up?"

"Unfortunately, No. He has all those monitors and Lines attached. He has to stay in the incubator for now."

"But he is in very good shape and will soon be transferred up to the nursery ward at the North Bay General Hospital." She said.

We spent the next few minutes talking to him and aweing and ooing and then the Nurse said: "Doctor Sharma" is out at the nurses station and would like to talk to you . . ." (He was the specialist that examined our baby for Fetal Alcohol Syndrome).

We both felt our stomachs tighten up as we weren't sure what this news would be but we knew we had to go and hear the Doctor out.

Doctor Sharma was one of those people you feel good about the minute you lay your eyes on them. He had a beaming smile and grabbed my hand immediately and asked: "You are Mr. & Mrs. Swartman??"

"Yes, Doctor". I said.

"Let me start right off by telling you that I have done extensive tests on that boy in there and there is no indication of Fetal Alcohol Syndrome. I think you are OK at this point but I will have to throw out one cautionary warning that I hope you take to heart."

"And what would that be Doc?" I asked.

He said: "Here's the thing. His birth mother was heavy into both alcohol and drugs. She may have abstained a great deal or partially during the pregnancy but all signs point to the fact that she may (or may not) be schizophrenic. If this is the case you need to keep a close eye on the boy. His mother witnessed a horrific accident with her younger brother as a child and it has scarred her mentally for life. At this point, he appears perfectly normal but problems will only surface, if any, later in life, teens or early twenties . . ."

"Thanks Doc. We really appreciate the heads up!"

And so we were done our first visit to our newest member of the family, who we would choose to name Jesse.

As we left the Neo-Natal Unit, the Head Nurse told us that "our boy" would be in the Nursery Ward at North Bay General Hospital in two days. We thanked her for all her help and Ann said: "You are right! He wins the baby beauty contest hands down!!"

We travelled back to North Bay and spent two restless days and nights waiting for our new family member to arrive in our territory.

Two days later Ann received a call from the North Bay General Hospital that our Jesse had arrived at the Nursery Ward. We asked when we could come visit him. The Nurse in the ward said whenever we were ready.

So we went as soon as I got home for work.

Our boy was in very good spirits and seemed to recognize us even though we had only seen him at CHEO a few days ago. Ann picked him up first and he smiled at her right away. She looked at me and beamed. It was love at first sight! She handed him over to me and I got a big grin too. I guess that was our approval stage.

We were told that the Children's Aid said we could take him home in three days after all tests results were back. So we came every day for a visit until the final day that we could take baby home.

On the big day we went to the Maternity Ward and took our new addition to the Swartman family. As we walked out of the hospital we noticed that one of my clients at the Caisse was mowing the hospital lawns. He said: "What you got there?"

I told him, "Dave we just adopted a newborn and we're taking him home today . . ."

"Isn't that a wonder. Can I see him?"

"Well yes, what do you think?"

Ann had him bundled up in a blanket with just the face showing. She walked over to Dave and said : "Here he is . . . We are going to call him Jesse!"

Dave said: "What a handsome young lad . . . . He even looks like you guys!"

CHAPTER 8

Meanwhile Back at the ranch

We got back home and Ann's Mom was ballistic so happy about Jesse. Peter not so much, still being kind of reserved. He never had a son and I guess he was afraid he might have a grandson but that might explode if the birth mother might renege on the deal. I was pretty certain that would never happen since if she didn't let us adopt the child he would automatically become a ward of the Children's aid.

30 days past. We are now going to have to go to Court to formalize our adoption, the change of name and get our certificate of adoption. The Judge was a very nice person who seemed to connect with us immediately and gave us this small lecture about the responsibilities of parenthood then stamped our application.

Ann's Aunt Esther . . . .

Ann's Aunt Esther had been following our adoption details as relayed to her by Ann's mother on a regular basis. She was extremely pleased that we were starting a family having been childless for over 18 years.

On the weekend after our court date, now that everything was officially finalized, Ann's mother, her Aunt Esther and her uncle Harold's partner Emily all came for a visit to see Jesse. As soon as her Aunt Esther saw the baby in the crib she burst out in tears and hugged Ann saying how happy she was for us and not to worry they are tears of joy.

Later that day we went over to Ann's parents and this time Peter not only picked Jesse he held him on his lap and even carried him around.

We invited them for supper the next night and advised them we would be cracking open a 20 year old bottle of champagne I had received from a customer in Ottawa many years ago. We had kept it for years waiting for a special occasion. Now we figured we had the perfect time for that.

CHAPTER 9

The following Monday morning, when we opened up the Head Office Courier bag, I had this sinking feeling. There was an announcement Memo that our Regional Manager had been transferred to New Brunswick as a Vice President. He was to be replaced by Robert Galipeau, the Senior Assistant Manager at the Ottawa Flagship Branch on Montreal Road. Both Galipeau and his Manager Gilles St.Cyr had applied for this job but they passed over St.Cyr in favour of Galipeau, which was not well received.

St.Cyr was a bit of a Dandy in that he dressed in extravagant suites one of which was pure white, with a white tie, socks and white shoes. Because of this he'd been nicknamed "Man from Glad" . No one dared call him that to his face as he had a bad temper. He also had a reputation of sexual harassment and had been the subject of several complaints from female employees to Human Resources Department. It was widely believed his history cost him that District Manager's promotion.

I wasn't pleased to hear that Galipeau had received this job. Several times he had approached me at Manager's meetings to transfer back to Ottawa and work at the Flagship Branch, for which I wasn't even remotely interested. Every time I declined his invitation he was visibly angered.

Now he would be coming to my Branch for periodic inspections. He had a reputation of being a real nit-picker.

At least he left me alone for a few months. There were many branches in the Eastern Ontario area that weren't functioning well, one that had been subjected to armed hold-ups three times in one year. And it was not profitable besides. What got all the Branch Managers upset is when they finally closed this Branch, they promoted the female Branch Manager who couldn't develop any business or achieve a profit, to the role of Assistant Manager in the Credit Department. Made no sense whatsoever.

I told my counterpart in Sudbury: "She wouldn't know a loan if she fell over it!"

Yet here we were, having to submit deals to her that were over our Branch limit. We all grinded our teeth on that one.

CHAPTER 10

Manager's Meeting in Ottawa

From time to time, all Branch Managers in Eastern and Northern Ontario Branches were called to Ottawa for an all-day "Information Meeting". Out of town Manager's more than 50 miles from Ottawa were told to come the night before. We would book a suite at Minto or Les Suites with 2 bedrooms. Then myself from North Bay, The Managers from Timmins and Sudbury would bunk in together.

All three of us were gourmet cooks and we'd take turns putting on a lavish meal that we prepared ourselves at less than half the price of Dining out at The Keg or Al's Steak house.

My friend Andre from Timmins would go out to the market and come back with three Filet Mignons which he would broil wrapped in bacon. Jacques from Sudbury went into the market and came back with Danish Lobster tails and Sea Scallops. One time I prepared Chicken Parmesan and served that with Pasta and Caesar Salad. We always ate well.

At our first such meeting with the newly minted Regional Manager he was in rare form. Robert Galipeau was a very high strung highly animated person and spoke with such intensity, he would unconsciously spit as he spoke excitedly. So I knew I would never sit beside or across from him. I told some of my collegues they should "keep a towel handy . . . you'll need it'.

On this occasion, our new boss gave the typical new boss speech about how he would work closely with his men and women and under his guidance we would achieve never before dreamed of volumes and profits.

Later in the morning, he introduced the newly appointed Senior Manager of the Commercial Credit Department. Her name was Manon St.Amand and was originally from the New Brunswick division. She had an MBA from Dorchester University and really plastered on the make-up. Down on the Byward Market she would easily have been taken for a prostitute given the make-up and the way she dressed.

Robert Galipeau left her alone with the twenty four Managers in the room and she laid out her action plan for her new position and her expectations of what she wanted from us in our Commercial Credit Submissions. At one point we all had to bite our tongues when she referred to "Accounts Receivable" on a corporation balance sheet as a liability. We wondered how she ever achieved an MBA much less get appointed to this job.

It turned out she was a full blown out of the closet Lesbian and was getting right into the groove of things already by joining up with the executive of the Ottawa Gay Pride Parade committee.

When the meeting ended we were left with the impression that she didn't have much use for male Branch Managers. Little did we know how this would eventually play out.

CHAPTER 11

Back in North Bay everything was back to normal. One of my first Commercial Applicants was a freshly minted Chiropractor fresh out of College. He wanted to open up a new practice but had been to three of the Banks in town and declined by all three. He was referred to me by Brad at CIBC as he told him I was more flexible with more discretionary authority than the other managers.

I was a thin application. He was heavily in debt Student Loans and no assets. However his Credit was excellent. His wife had just been hired as a full-time RN at the North Bay District Hospital so there was decent family income even if his was slow during business start-up. I personally liked him and my gut feeling was he would be very successful with his outgoing personality and aggressive marketing ideas and plans.

His father-in-law was a local High School Principal, so I approved him for a small credit line (with his Father-in Law's Letter of Guarantee) and a government guaranteed Small Business Improvement Loan to purchase his equipment and do some Leasehold improvements. I advised him, I'd drop his father-in-Law's Guarantee as soon as he produced a one year Financial Statement showing a profitable practice.

He was extremely grateful and invited me to the grand opening at which he insisted on bragging about me to the North Bay Nugget and even have his picture taken with me for that article. At first I wasn't crazy about the idea, but later when I got two more brand new Commercial clients as spinoff from the article I was pretty pleased with the outcome.

CHAPTER 12

SOME OF THESE HEAD OFFICE PEOPLE AREN'T SO PERFECT . . .

Yet another Manager's Meeting two months later at the Golf Course at Gananoque, Ontario. This was a command performance as we were to be treated to the company of non other than the Chief Executive Officer and our Senior Executive Vice President. There was no such thing as an excuse why couldn't attend (only if you were in Intensive Care on Life support).

All the Head office big wigs were there. There was the Manager, Commercial Credit and his equals from Mortgages and Consumer Credit. There were the Managers of Human Resources, Premises and Operations. The Manager of Premises was a very strange person (back then he would be referred to as a nerd). His features were quite pronounced as his face seemed to develop into a V shape much like a rat. He was extremely tight on approving new equipment or getting improvements done in a branch such as replacing old worn out desks or filing cabinets. He wasn't well liked and he developed the nickname of "Rodentious.P.Premises".

The other person not so well liked by Branch Managers was the Manager Human Resources. His was the job of signing off on everyone's Annual Performance Appraisal. He was also the one who with the Regional Vice President decided who was to be promoted, demoted and fired.

The meeting was an all morning affair starting with breakfast and non-stop speeches and presentations until early afternoon. Then there was a light lunch followed by eighteen rounds of Golf for those so inclined. My two sidekicks from Timmins and Sudbury were not interested so we adjourned to the games room for back to back games on the pool tables of Boston and Snooker.

This was the day that the Manager, Human Resource had a major fall from grace. He had been drinking out on the Golf Course, then again at the nineteenth hole. Then he kept on going during the dinner. At one point before dessert he excused himself and staggered off to the bathroom. And no one seemed to notice that he didn't return.

Ultimately, he passed out sitting on the toilet in the Men's washroom. No one noticed him in the end stall of a series of twelve stalls. He woke up finally at three o'clock in the morning in the pitch black. Everyone had gone home and turned off the lights and shut down the golf course. When he finally got his bearings and realized his predicament it took quite a few phone calls to get someone to come and rescue him. We all really enjoyed his misery.

MEANWHILE BACK AT THE BRANCH

I received a call from Robert Galipeau's Secretary advising me that our Regional Manager was coming up for his first Branch visit and should be checking into the Holiday Inn at about 10:00 p.m.that night. Did I want to meet with him for a cocktail? I declined the invitation explaining to her that I was on my way to bed at that time of night. She then told me Monsieur Galipeau would expect to meet me at 7:30 a.m. in the restaurant at Holiday Inn so we could "breakfast" together. I said: "Sounds fine to me!"

Breakfast was the usual Regional Manager/Branch Manager start of the day conversation. Been there done that before. He laid out his schedule: tour the Branch, meet all the staff during the day, look at all my recent loans granted in my limit, decide if he should increase my limit if he liked my judgment to date, have a staff meeting after closing where he would address all the staff including me. Then he would leave and head back to Ottawa after the Branch closed.

This was not a fun day. I've seen nitpickers in my life but this man took the cake. He would walk into our vault and run his finger across the top of the safety deposit nest to see if the cleaners had left any dust. He couldn't find any dust in the Branch anywhere but just had to comment on the fact that our cleaner had neglected to remove a miniscule cobweb in a high ceiling corner that you would need a magnifying glass to locate, so I better had to have a talk with this cleaner right away.

Yessir. I'll get right on to that.

Then he looked at my loans. Overall he was pretty pleased with not only the volume but the quality of my loan approvals. But I had committed the ultimate sin in his mind. I had approved a Loan for a "Chip Wagon". Never mind it was guaranteed by one of the richest businessmen in North Bay, this was not good business.These Chip Wagons had a high failure rate and we would end up asking our valued rich client to pay out this loan in the future thereby souring our relationship. I explained that in our Market Chip wagons survived and prospered. The residents of North Bay just loved their French Fries and Poutine!

He said in his thick French accent: "Just the same Leslie, NO MORE LOANS FOR DEM CHIP WAUGGANS!!"

The next morning I received a very favourable Branch Review and a form stating he was raising my Branch Lending Limit to $35,000 unsecured from $20,000, my Secured Limit to $75,000 from $50,000 and my Mortgage Limit to $150,000Conventional and my CMHC Insured Mortgage Limit to $500,000. Wow. I didn't think I made that good of an impression, but maybe I wasn't reading my new boss as good as I could.

Unfortunately, although we ended up getting along really well, He was only on this job for a year, then got transferred to Boca Ratan Florida as the New VP, Florida US operations. We now got a new VP from Montreal. His name was Jean-Pierre Graveline and he was quite a change. He never visited a Branch. It was all phone calls and "conference calls". He became very tight with our new Lesbian Manager of Commercial Lending Centre.

One of the first things he decided was that my Branch secretary would be re-allocated to our in Branch Commercial Lending Officer, Jennifer O'Grady. I had groomed Jennifer from a shy nervous assistant accountant all the way up to learning Commercial Lending and analyzing Company Financial Statements and preparing Commercial Loan presentations to take the heat off me so I would be able to run the Branch Operations and the Consumer Credit and Investment Departments. I didn't see it at the time, but this was the first little thin edge of the wedge of our newly minted Manager of the Commercial Lending Centre's assault on male Branch Managers.

Every year in June it was traditional that the Regional Manager would do the Annual Performance Appraisal of all the Branch Managers in the Region. This year I had a great P.A. as usual. Normally I would get the full raise allocated to all or most of the Managers with good results and profitability. This year was different in that Graveline called me and explained: "We only have so much in this year's envelope, Leslie. Your pay increase this year will be confined to half of one percent!"

I could almost feel him smiling on the other end of the phone. I said: "Well by the time you take deductions of that it won't even take me to the grocery store . . ."

"Are you complaining Swartman?" he asked. "No Sir, I guess something is better than nothing . . ." I let it go at that.

There was two things going against me at this point. Number one, my name was way too anglicized for many of the Management in the Caisse, regardless of my results. Number two, Graveline had got all chummy with Manon St.Amand who wasn't a big fan of mine as we had a few verbal run-ins over my Credit Files from time to time. So I kept my mouth shut.

CHAPTER 13

THOSE LOVELY BRANCH AUDITS

Another example of how my name wasn't my greatest asset showed up during every Branch Inspection. These took place every two to three years. If there was six members of the inspection teams, I would be lucky if even one of them spoke some broken English. Regardless of how good our Branch results were, it seemed like they were either on some kind of ego trip or just plain miserable. Seventy five percent of these inspectors were fresh out of University with their MBA, never worked in a Branch yet, never dealt with the public and had limited life experience. Nevertheless they felt they were experts in every sense.

One such inspector arrived for the second time in our Branch, having been a rookie on the team three years prior. Now he was the Senior Team Leader. On the previous inspection he had reamed me out for a loan I had made to an unemployed factory worker. Now he had never made a loan in his life and at this point I had been lending money for 18 years. I tried to explain to him about character analysis and gut feelings but he wouldn't hear of it. He rated it the worst rating he could give and predicted it would someday be a total write off to the Branch. At the time I told him to come back in two or three years and we'll see who knows a loan and who doesn't. Of course that didn't sit well and he got his boss at the time to write up some negative comments about me in the inspection summary.

At my very first opportunity, I pulled out my clients file and invited him into my office. **"Remember this Loan, Gaston?"** I asked. **"Not sure."** He said.

So I handed him his comments from his previous inspection to refresh his memory.

"Now here's the thing, Gaston. In the last three years, this customer has never missed a payment. I had put him on an interest only demand loan while he was on UIC, so he could afford to live and feed his family. Three months into this loan he was hired by DND at CFB North Bay, making better money than he had at his previous job that laid him off. I switched him to blended payment and he's doing just fine. In fact he appreciated us so much, he transferred all his RRIF's to us from his previous job. His mother passed away and he invested the entire estate here at the Caisse. It's all in the fact of knowing your client, Gaston.."

This time around Gaston was much gentler on the inspection.

BRANCH OF THE YEAR

Our new Regional V.P. decided he would start to have contests each year in the Region. So the Branch with the best results judged by volume increase in loans and deposits, no customer complaints and other Head office reports, there would be an annual Manager's meeting where the winning Branch would receive a beautiful engraved plaque from Vice-President J.P.Graveline.

North Bay Branch won it twice in the 90's and it must have had Monsieur Graveline grinding his teeth to have to present this to "Swartman" . . . . .He couldn't get around it. Head office printouts put us as the number 24th most efficient Branch in all of Canada. In Ontario the Divisional Vice President rated North Bay Branch in the top ten most profitable Branches in the province. We had even beaten out the big "Flagship Branch" in Ottawa!

TIME MARCHES ON

The Age of Technology hit the Banking business like a sledgehammer. At first everyone was advised to become familiar with computers. They would be the way of the future. They started by giving out employees miniature game computers which was to get us used to the keyboard. Then they advised that ATM's (Automated Teller Machines) were just around the corner. I guess the Branch tellers (now titled CSR's= Customer Service

Representatives) should have clued in that something not nice lied ahead on the horizon. Some did others didn't.

So then we Branch Managers were summoned to Ottawa for an "Your Ears Only" meeting. This was a meeting that explained how not only the Caisse but all the Banks had developed a new computer programme/platform that measures profitability but most importantly return on Investment (ROI) to the Banks shareholders. This was the most important aspect of the Banks operations and new rules were to be applied throughout the entire Bank so that the ROI could be maximized for their precious shareholders. What about the employees? Nada. Shareholder returns were to be the number one priority. Hence a new term was coined: "Restructuring".

What did Restructuring involve? Well the first part of Restructuring was to revise that fulltime employees that were 37.5 hours per week with full benefits were to be re-assigned to less than 30 hours per week so they wouldn't qualify for benefits. Accept it or else.

The one good thing is that I didn't have to initially as a Branch Manager have to deliver these Messages to my employees. Their Head Office HR people and VP's did the dirty work in an early morning Branch staff meeting complete with coffee and donuts from Tim Horton's. However I had to clean up the fall out. When you had to explain to Suzy that she was being reduced from full-time status to part-time, losing her benefits and a reduction in salary even though she had excellent performance appraisals forever, this was not a fun thing. We were told we had to tow the line on the head office's branding of this thing called "restructuring". In the long run it would keep the Bank profitable and serve our clients better!

On top of this they decided as part of "restructuring" the title Branch Manager was to be replaced by "Team Leader". I was informed I could choose between being an "Area Regional Manager" or move to Ottawa and be a "Commercial Account Manager". If I chose to be an "Area Regional Manager" then I would continue to be in charge of the Branch in North Bay, but also be in charge of five Northern Ontario Branches. And I would have to close two of the least profitable branches of the five, eliminating the least productive employees of these branches and then eliminating the least productive employees in the remaining three branches and replacing them from the two cancelled branches. No thanks! And no thanks moving to Ottawa and doing Commercial Loans 7/24.

This did not enamour me to our new VP.

So the next thing was I started to get the cold shoulder. Not just me but my equal in Kingston Ontario. He was also an Anglophone and didn't speak a word of French. On Conference Calls between the VP and the Branch Managers, he would have start off "en francaise" and I'd have to say: **"Monsieur Graveline! The Kingston Manager can't understand this call!" "Oh oui, excusez-moi!"** And the call would go back to English for the remainder . . .

The farther up the ladder you get the more rapid the turnover. Or as one previous Manager once told me: **"Da higher you get in da Bank, da closer you are to da door!"**

Just when I thought things couldn't get much worse, We are notified by way of a Head Office Memo to all branches that our V.P. J.P.Graveline was being promoted to Vice-President of Credit Card Services for all of Canada, He would be moving to Montreal. His replacement wasn't named yet.

CHAPTER 14

GUESS WHO IS THE NEW BOSS!

Next came the worst phone call of my life. Our secretary asked me to take Line one, Manon St.Amand was on the line. She had this very phony friendly voice that was instantly irritating. **"Hi der Lezzlee! I got very important news for you and your Team! I will be replacing J.P Graveline as the new Regional Vice Prezeedent!"**

I wished her congratulations. Then she said she had many calls to make and would get back to me soon to plan her next Branch visit.

Apparently, our new VP had this agenda. She wanted to put in her PA (performance appraisal) that she had promoted many female Branch Managers thereby raising the level of female Branch Managers under her watch. Unfortunately this came at the expense of the elimination of existing productive Male Branch Managers.

The first one was the Manager of the Flagship Branch on Rideau Street in Ottawa. The Assistant Manager was a female who incidentally was romantically involved on an ACDC relationship with VP Manon. The Male Manager was found to be sexually harassing the female employees (unfounded) but was dismissed summarily and never got his job back.

Next the Manager in Kingston was replaced (even though he was very popular with the clientele) and was replaced by another of VP Manon's lesbian lovers who wasn't and never had been even a Branch Manager in Eastern Ontario.

So now it was my turn.

At first they decided to try the old "creative dismissal" plan. I would first be demoted from Branch Manager for the last 20 years to the Regional

Marketing Manager. They didn't have a job description for this job but I was to design it for HR.. I would leave my Manager's office I had occupied for 20 years so my former Assistant Manager that I had groomed from a wimpy blushing assistant accountant to a Commercial Account Manager because she was now appointed to take over my Branch. She would be given the title of "Team Leader"

At one time, our VP Manon came from Sudbury to our Branch during our latest Audit. I knew she was in Sudbury during the day with her latest squeeze the Vice President of Desjardins Mutual Funds, her buddy on the Gay Pride Parade Committee.

She was very late arriving, her clothes were all wrinkled and her makeup smeared. I had to call home twice and finally told Ann go ahead and eat supper, I'll be there when I get there.

She hardly spoke to me, spending all her time with the inspectors upstairs in the lunch room.

As she left with the inspectors she said I could close up the Branch now and she'd be back soon to do my 'annual review' . . . . .

My old fishing buddy had taken on the job I didn't want as Area Branch Manager. About three weeks later they arrived on a Tuesday to meet with me for a head to head in the staff Lunch room. Manon came up the night before and stayed at the Holiday Inn, so she could invite the newly appointed Branch female Team Leader over for a few drinks and whatever.

It was a good thing I have a great memory. Some of the statements made to me by this incompetent VP was making my old fishing buddy blush. She started off by saying: **"I didn't realize you were dat old Lezlie!!"** So I said: **"Oh, do you consider 55 old?"** Then she said : **"Lezlie, do you realize you are one of the most highest paid Managers in dis Region?"** To this I said: **"Maybe that's why I'm the most profitable Branch in your region and one of the ten most profitable Branches in Ontario?"** This seemed to make her angry and she terminated the interview and left.

After that I went for a walk with my (whom I thought) was my buddy and he said: "Manon wants to put an ad in the North Bay Nugget stating that Jennifer has been appointed as the new Branch Manager." To which I said: **"Well then what is this bullshit that they've changed the title of Branch Manager to Team Leader? How do you think the clients in North Bay will react to this?"**

"You got a point there . . ."

Then after we got back to the branch I wrote down a word for word account of this meeting as I knew Manon wouldn't have the brainpower to cover her ass.

CHAPTER 15

LET'S END THIS AGONY ONCE AND FOR ALL!

Then the day came. I had been doing this made up job that I had wrote the job description for that HR wouldn't even acknowledge. On top of that I had been training staff for the February RRSP campaign which we not only met but exceeded our goals.

Before the (let's call it a) demotion it was part of my job to rally the troops every year during the RRSP campaigns. Which we did exceedingly well. Every year either met or exceeded our Campaign Objectives. I was always playing tricks on my girls in the Branch, one of which was the ultimate practical joke.

I was always the first person in most mornings to open up the Branch. My Branch Accountant was usually second in and usually swamped with paperwork. One morning about 8:30 a.m. before the rest of the staff arrived I picked up line three and dialed line one. Sophie, my Branch Accountant saw I was on the phone so answered line one.

The conversation went something like this:

"Caisse Populaire, this is Sophie, how can I help you?" I then put on my best Chinese accent and said: **"This is Doctor Wun Hung Lo. I work at Atomic Industy Plant. I look for best intwest late on ah ah ss pee! What yo late?? For five yee-ah pran??"**

"Well Mr. Lo . . . ." **"DAT DOCTOR HUNG LO!** **"I'm sorry Doctor Hung Lo, Our current best five year rate would be 3.95 % . . . ."** At this point I upped the volume, slightly angry tone of voice . . .

"DAT ALL? YOU GOT LOW LATES!! TONTO MINION GOT BEDDA LATES DAN YOU GUYS!!!"

Just then Sophie spun around in her chair and looked straight at me . . . I said: **"Hi Sophie are you getting some business out of that Doctor Hung Lo or what?"**

"Oh Leslie!!! You are so bad!! You really had me going there . . . shame on you!" Then we both had a good laugh.

Or then there was another dandy two years previous: It was a Friday night the final day of that year's RRSP campaign, February 28th. We had closed down the Branch and were leaving at 6:10 p.m. As Sophie locked the door to the Branch, she said: **"I'm so glad this year's RRSP campaign is over. I never want to hear that friggin' word for a long time!"** "What word is that Sophie?" I asked. **"Well, RRSP of course!!"** She said.

A light bulb came on over my head. Monday morning I am in the Branch early. I'm making up little sticky notes and plastering them all over the Branch. They read: GOT YOUR RRSP YET??? and RRSP'S ARE THE GREATEST!! and YOU NEED YOUR RRSP RIGHT NOW!! I put one on her phone, one above the combination dial she had to spin on the Vault door. Another on the mirror in the girl's washroom. The last one in her desk on top her supply of Bank blank forms. She pretended to be angry at first, then burst out laughing. Moreso everytime she discovered a new sticker. Those were fun times.

But that was then and this was now.

I had to suffer the borderline insult comments from my Commercial Clients who wouldn't be in business if I hadn't approved them years previous, but now they'd be sucking up to Jennifer because I wasn't doing Commercial anymore. Boy did they get a big surprise on their next annual review!

So I got a call from my former fishing buddy about 3:00 p.m. **"Hi Les? How's the day going?"** "Pretty much usual man. Like the last time we spoke . . . my guts are churning steady everyday wondering what's the next great surprise in store from Ottawa."

"I'm in North Bay right now at Traveller's Inn. Can you come by after work, say about 4:30 . . . Five'ish?" "I need to meet with you today after work, Les. I said: " **Wild horses couldn't keep me away, man!"**

THE BIG EXIT INTERVIEW

I walked in to the main Lobby of Travellers Inn and there was Harry my old fishing buddy looking very nervous indeed. I walked up to him and shook his hand. My hand was dry, his was soaked with sweat. I had already figured out what this was all about, but the sweaty hands confirmed my thoughts. He said let's go up to my room. Up on the second floor we walked in and there was Angeline Labelle from HR in Ottawa. She was new in the job and looked even more freaked out than Harry. After all, you don't fire a Senior Branch Manager everyday?

I felt sorry for Harry. He was actually stuck with the job of eliminating my position because the Regional Vice President was a gutless wonder and had delegated the job to him. She called him the day before and said she was stuck in meetings in Montreal with the Senior Brass so he'd have to take care of dispatching Leslie up in North Bay. **"Dat's part of da job Harry, Okay?"**

Of course there was this preplanned order for the meeting whereby they would explain what was going down and my options. It went something like this:

Harry started off with this: **"We are here today to discuss our current restructuring in this District and how it affects North Bay Branch. Angeline who you know is here representing HR Dept. and I as you know represent the District and our Regional Vice President."** At this point I gave them my best I couldn't give a shit look.

"To cut to the chase, Leslie the position you now fill has been eliminated in this Branch and we are prepared to offer you this exit package". At this point he shoved a bunch of papers across the table to me. After I leafed through them I knew this was a poker game that HR usually won. While I was pretty high strung I didn't go directly into stupid mode and start signing this paperwork.

I looked at Harry and said: **"Down there in Ottawa they must take me for a complete fool to make me an offer like this? Tell them to stick this deal where the sun don't shine."**

Harry said: **"You are not required to sign anything today, but we do need for you to acknowledge today that we made you this offer"**. He then shoved a paper at me which I read carefully and the long and short of it was they were offering me one week of pay for each year of service. This was one third of Industry norms. I didn't have to sign acceptance of their offer, just another form acknowledging the fact that they had made the offer and I declined to accept. I signed his copy and kept mine. He then suggested that we go to the Branch so I could clean out my desk. The Branch staff had all left for the day.

I said: **"Let's get this over with I'll meet you at the Branch in about 15 minutes"** ....

I left the hotel and went down to my client's Restaurant. He had a Bank of payphones outside the washrooms. So I called home to Anne.

When she answered the phone I told her all my suspicions were 100 per cent confirmed. They were putting me out to pasture. I told her about the ridiculous offer they had made and how I had to go to the Branch and "clean out my desk"(one of the most horrific expressions in the Banking business!). I told her I didn't know when I'd be home but go ahead and eat with our son as I don't think I'll have much of an appetite tonight ....

Now it was time to head to the Branch. When I arrived there was Jennifer standing behind what used to be my desk. The second she saw me she turned her reddening face to the wall just like any traitor would have done. I went to my office where Harry was waiting and proceeded to empty out my personal contents into the cardboard box they were so good to provide. I took down the two Branch of the Year plaques and told Harry: **"Why don't you ask Manon for me to take these and stick them up her ass?"**

He was trying hard to look business like but a ghost of a smile flickered for a minute. After all. He hated her just as much as everyone else, but they all had to suck up to her to keep their jobs. Some were getting close to retirement!

So I left. I went home, stomach churning all the way. I had to stop before my gate and get out of the car so I could do the "dry heaves" .... Nothing in my stomach to throw up other than saliva and stomach acid.

I couldn't even look at food, so I had a couple of "hot toddies"to help me sleep. We talked the subject to death for about two hours, then I hit the sack.

CHAPTER 16

NEXT MORNING DIFFERENT STORY

When I got up the next morning, the sun was shining and the coffee was strong and I decided that maybe my former employer was going to wear this one.

I made a few calls and was recommended to a "Labour Litigation Law Firm" in Ottawa. I even got a name and they said his middle name should be "BARRACUDA!" I loved it. I made an appointment. I decided to take my son along and we parked in a parking lot on Gloucester Street as The Law Firm was on Metcalfe. As we were making our way to the Office building there were two homeless people in front of a house beside the building we were about to enter. The homeless lady was wearing a dress and proceeded to pull down her panties and squat to urinate in the some homeowners small garden. She shouted at me: **"Don't Look!!"** I shielded my son's face a stepped up our pace immediately.

My Lawyer was about six foot six inches tall and had a lean build. I handed him a briefcase which contained all my recent performance appraisals, Branch profitability reports, Memos from VP's congratulating me as well as notes taken at all recent meetings with Manon.

My new lawyer said: **"I wish all my clients were as well prepared as you . . . The Caisse Pop are going to hate you and me by the time I'm through with them."**

He then advised me to file for Unemployment Insurance right away. I was to advise him when I had accomplished this. Meanwhile, I decided maybe I'd had enough of the Banking Industry. Who would hire a 55 year old anyway? I had held my nose and applied for a position at the Bank of

Montreal. It was a lady Branch Manager and I could see her and I would be like fire and water, just from the way she talked down to her employees. Not too many smiling faces in that Branch. I withdrew my application.

I was counselled to hunker down, my Lawyer was going after a juicy settlement. There would be a lot of resistance at first so this could drag on for months. Meanwhile I decided I'd get back into Financial Services. I was informally recruited by Great West Life (my Lawyer advised me to keep that under the radar) and took the next few weeks to recertify myself for Life, Health, Disabilty Insurance licences as well as re-instate my Mutual Funds License. All the time I was studying for these courses, the Government of Canada were paying me Unemployment Insurance Benefits "the dole" (the first time I'd ever collected in my entire life and after 37 years in the workforce).

The summer passed quickly and in late August, I received a call from Mr. John Barracuda, Q.C. He said: **"Believe it or not, we did it! Here's your deal. We've tripled your original cash payout offer. They have to pay all my fees (worth about $8000). They have to pay for any employment counselling or training courses to a maximum of $5000. And finally they have to write a real nicey nicey Letter of Recommendation stating what a wonderful employee you were, your Branch of the year awards, great profitability, etc. He said you could almost hear them grinding their teeth, when I finally got them to agree to all this rather than go to court".** He chuckled. **"I need you down here to sign all the settlement documents as soon as possible."**

Since this was a Friday I asked if it was OK to come down the following Monday. We agreed on a time and ended our talk.

In about a week I received a letter in the mail from the Caisse Head Office from the HR Department. In it was my letter of recommendation. As I read it I could almost hear them in HR grinding their teeth as they composed this against their will, but no choice . . . part of the settlement Mr. Barracuda squeezed out of them.. It went like this:

To Whom it May Concern

Re: Letter of Reference for Leslie Swartman

Leslie Swartman was employed by Caisse Populaire for just under twenty years. He served as the Branch Manager of our North Bay Branch prior to the elimination of his position due to restructuring.

Mr. Swartman made significant contributions to the growth and development of the Caisse Populaire's presence within the North Bay community, showing himself to be a valuable, conscientious and professional Manager. The North Bay Branch was chosen as the Caisse Populaire Branch of the year under Mr. Swartman's leadership and guidance. Most recently the North Bay Branch last year was included amongst the Caisse's top twenty five most efficient branches out of hundreds of Branches in Canada. His was the only Branch in Ontario to achieve this distinction.

Mr. Swartman possesses outstanding abilities to manage, to provide advice and to solve problems. He was a highly regarded and respected Branch Manager within the Bank and amongst his clients, his employees and the North Bay community at large. We wish Mr. Swartman well in his future endeavours and would have no hesitation in recommending for any role which would allow him an opportunity to utilize his considerable managerial skills and experience in the financial services industry.

Sincerely,
CAISSE POPULAIRE DESJARDINS
Jeanne D'arc Plouffe,
Manager, Employee Relations

CHAPTER 17

PORTABLE SKILLS TO TAKE ANYWHERE

I recall that I was at a Training Seminar in Montreal one time at The Caisse Head Office. The Instructor was very dynamic and highly motivated unlike most instructors. The most memorable statement he had come out with during our training course was about moving through more than one career in life. He noted how the previous generation used to start in a career when young and stay in that field for decades until retirement. But in our generation we acquired basic skills like Credit Judgement, Investment Counselling skills and knowledge of financial products that we could port with us to different employers and companies.

And so it panned out this way with Great West Life. I started out as a recruit and besides taking my Head Office Training which lasted over a six week period, I prepared myself for my certification exams for Life Insurance, Group Health and Disability Licenses.

When the day came to write my exams in the late fall, there were thirty men and women in the room and an older lady and I were the first two to complete both exams and turn them in and head for the door. I had learned years ago: bypass the questions you aren't one hundred percent sure of. Do all the easy ones quickly then come back and work on the harder ones, using common sense. As a result I achieved marks of 95% on the Life Exam and 87% on Group Health and Disability exams.

There were two other Agents in North Bay for GWL (Great West Life)and they'd carved out a large portion of the market. It was explained that I can go after potential clients that aren't GWL, but I couldn't "mow their grass".

At first I was on a draw against Commissions, much less take home than when at the Caisse, but we adjusted. Neither one of the other Agents were familiar with mortgages and this allowed me to go aggressively after the Mortgage business and also do their clients mortgages when a need was identified. I went after my old Caisse mortgage clients with a vengeance doing straight transfers and refinances to our Mortgage Division GWM (Great West Mortgages).

In fact I did so well in my first year I did 55% of all mortgage business out of seventy Agents in Eastern and Northern Ontario. The Manager of GWM sent me the largest fruit basket I've ever seen with a warm Thank You Note signed by all the Underwriters and Management staff at GWM Head Office in Guelph.

But I was quickly learning that maybe I should rethink about how I want to spend my time. North Bay was besieged with Life Insurance Agents, Investment Agents and the competition was fierce. I had a former Commercial client that I'd set up in business years previous. I'd seen him through some rough periods as he established himself against the North Bay competition in his field. Now that I was no longer the Manager of the Bank (Caisse) he begrudgingly agreed to let me do a proposal to him and his Common Law spouse over which I laboured for many hours. One night I made the presentation to them. At one point he appeared to be wanting to look macho and protecting his gal pal from the big bad Investment Companies. I was told: **"We'll get back to you".**

WHAT HAVE YOU DONE FOR ME LATELY??

A few days later my former and unappreciative Bank client called me and told me that he had Robert Dick, another Investment Counsellor who worked for Investors Syndicate had reviewed my in-depth presentation and tore it to pieces, and came up with a better plan. **"Of course he did"**, I said. **"Whaddya mean, Leslie?"** he asked.

I said: **"It doesn't take much talent to take some one else's work and do a major critique of it especially if the end result is you will receive a commission cheque. He will put you and your girlfriend into the flavour of the month that earns him the biggest bucks. My plan was taking into account your spouse's obvious risk aversion. Anyway you go with Mr.Dick and let me know in a year or to if you are ahead** or behind. **Anyway, thanks for letting me offer you my company's service and our personalized plan and I wish you the best. No hard feelings."**

He seemed quite embarrassed momentarily, but I thanked him in my best friendly and professional tone of voice and hung up feeling good about the conversation.

That night I received the call that I needed at that point in my life. My old comrade from the Caisse called me to recruit me to his current employer. He had really been jerked by Manon and after they packaged him off he went into a major depression. Fortunately, he had been given the option in his exit package to get "Career Counselling" from a professional firm. He took this up and was informed he was the perfect candidate to be a Mortgage Consultant! So he was hired immediately by Mortgage Advantage Inc. Within months he was making way more money than he ever earned at the Caisse. In fact a year later he told me: **"Hey Les! Last week I went to our Hyundai Dealer here in Kingston and bought me a brand new Hyundai Tiboron. And I wrote them a cheque for it!"** I said: **"No shit!"**

He suggested I apply to the BDM (Business Development Manager) through the Mortgage Advantage Website and send them my up to date resume. Which I did. The very next day I got a call from Mr. Ted Wilson, the BDM. He asked was there any way I could come to Ottawa and Meet him at Les Suites in the Byward Market on the following Friday as he would be in Ottawa that day and would like to interview me along with the Ottawa "Team Leader" for a new Mortgage Consultant position for the North Bay/Northern Ontario Market. I agreed. Maybe they'd want me, maybe not.

Friday came. I was to meet them at 11:00 a.m. in the lobby of Les Suites. We identified each other immediately as you can spot a Banker or ex-Banker pretty quick. With Ted Wilson sat this gorgeous Lebanese woman in her early thirties who reminded me of a taller version of Paula Abdul but much more business-like. I was introduced to Sandra Zahab, who would be my new boss in the mortgage business if I was hired. I could see early on the chemistry was right between all three of us.

The meeting concluded and Wilson advised me that: **"They would be in touch with me soon with our decision . . ."**

As I shook hands with them before leaving I noticed Sandra winked at me. The wink was worth a thousand words.

THE MORTGAGE BUSINESS

My next career in life was probably my favourite. Team Ottawa started out as six Mortgage Agents. We moved from our first company twice to achieve better commission deals and benefits. And most of all better autonomy. We shed three of the original six along the way and nowadays it's Sandra, Sylvianne (consistently one of the top producers in Canada) and Leslie. We are the original "Three Mortgage Mouseketeers"!

It reminds me of a pearly words of wisdom once bestowed to me by a silver haired TD Bank Branch Manager who asked me: **"Les, what's the definition of success?"** Before I could guess he told me: **"Success is having a job you love every day and getting paid for it!"**

I believe that's where we can get if we keep a positive mental attitude, put our portable skills to work always do today and look forward to tomorrow and to hell with their "Creative Dismissal".

THE END

www.ingramcontent.com/pod-product-compliance
Lightning Source LLC
Chambersburg PA
CBHW021024180526
45163CB00005B/2105